Reclaiming Your Time
Mindfulness and Time Management Strategies

Table of Contents

Chapter 1. Introduction

Welcome to a life-transforming Special Report titled, "Reclaiming Your Time: Mindfulness and Time Management Strategies." This captivating report is not just another document; it's a gateway towards reclaiming command over your life, through time. In an age where every minute counts, understanding how to best use your time significantly affects your personal and professional life. Delve into the secrets of marrying mindfulness and time management as we guide you through scientifically-proven strategies brimming with potential to not only enhance productivity but also amplify peace of mind. This is your resource, your compass towards making every tick-tock count, not with stress and pressure, but with joy and spaciousness. Unleash the power of now and step into a world where time is no longer fleeting, but a friend. Take control, stay cheerfully productive, and inject serene mindfulness into your daily routine. By the end of this Special Report, time will have transformed from constraint to ally; it's the magic waiting to happen!

Chapter 2. Understanding Time: Perception vs. Reality

At the intersection of philosophy and physics, the understanding of time is a complex topic. How we perceive time in our minds can often differ greatly from its objective reality. Let's take a detailed look at time, from our perception of it to the science that defines its existence.

2.1. The Process of Perception

The human condition is deeply rooted in the perception of time. Our routine activities, from sleeping to eating, are regulated by internal body clocks, also called circadian rhythms. The mechanism of this internal clock and how it influences our perception of time is a fascinating journey into the realms of neurobiology and psychology.

Our brain measures time, albeit inaccurately, through the sequential firing of neural circuits. This neural firing enables us to perceive the passage of time, the duration of an event, and even the time between two events. However, the perception influenced by these cerebral timekeepers is highly subjective. It can be altered by factors such as age, emotions, attention, and drugs. For instance, time can feel like it's flying when we're engrossed in an activity. Conversely, it can seem to drag when we're waiting for something.

2.2. Objective Reality of Time

Unlike our subjective perception, the physical reality of time is consistent and mathematically precise. Time, according to physics, is defined as the progression of events from the past through the present to the future. This linear and unidirectional flow of time is a fundamental construct of our physical universe.

Einstein's theory of relativity brought forth a stunning revelation - time is not absolute but relative, varying with the observer's motion and gravitational field. This science-backed concept of time, through its exactitude and invariance, starkly contrasts our often skewed perception of it.

2.3. The Perception-Reality Gap

The gap between our perception of time and its physical reality can lead to misunderstandings, missed opportunities, and stress. When we misjudge time, we often make poor decisions that impact our productivity and peace of mind adversely.

Understanding this perception-reality divide is critical to effectively managing our time. If we study and acknowledge the impacts of our perception on our utilization of time, we can take steps to align our perceived time with its objective reality.

2.4. Bridging The Gap

Studies suggest that our perception of time can be trained and aligned more closely with its quantitative reality. Here are a few ways this alignment can be done:

1. Regular schedule: Setting a routine aligns our circadian rhythms with the day-night cycle, reducing temporal illusions and increasing our productivity and satisfaction.

2. Mindful Attention: Being fully present in each moment can significantly enhance our accuracy in estimating the time an activity will require.

3. Reduce Multitasking: Juggling multiple tasks at once can distort our perception of time. Focusing on a single task at a time can make our estimation of time more accurate.

4. Exposure to nature: Various studies suggest that exposure to

natural environments can reset our internal clocks and enhance our time-perception accuracy.

By diligently applying these strategies, we can better approximate the physical reality of time in our perceptions and ultimately improve our time management skills.

2.5. Recalibrating Your Perception

The human brain is incredibly plastic and capable of learning new things throughout life. By persistently attempting to meet the objective reality of time with our perception, we can train ourselves to perceive time more accurately.

This recalibration is not just about increasing productivity; it's also a pathway to mindfulness. When we perceive time accurately, we tend to live more in the present, acknowledging each moment as it passes. This heightened awareness of 'now' is the essence of mindfulness.

In summary, understanding the nuances of time – both its subjective perception and objective reality, is imperative to develop effective time management skills. By recognizing the disparity between our mind's perception of time and its physical existence, we can strategize accordingly to lead a more productive, fulfilling and peaceful life. Remember, time is a resource that, unlike any other, once spent, cannot be regenerated. So, let's understand it, manage it wisely, and make every moment count!

Chapter 3. Mindful Approach: The Crucial First Step

Understanding the importance of the mindful approach in time management is crucial to setting the foundation towards taking control of your day. Mindfulness is more than just a buzzword; it's a methodology steeped in centuries of practice with scientifically proven benefits relevant to our modern, fast-paced lives. This chapter explores the significance, techniques, and direct results of merging mindfulness with time management.

3.1. The Intersection of Mindfulness and Time Management

Mindfulness, at its core, is deliberate attention to the present moment. It means being fully vested in whatever you're doing - not thinking about what's gone by, nor planning for the future, but experiencing every sensation attributed to the 'now.' Time management, on the other hand, is the strategic allocation of time resources to enhance productivity and efficiency. The intersection of these two principles leads to conscious control over moments, resulting in productive, meaningful, and fulfilling days.

When we're mindful, we're more receptive to our priorities and consequently better positioned to manage and allocate our time efficiently. For example, consider a common situation – working on a task while distracted by thoughts of the next. This scenario breeds mistakes and affects overall productivity. But, being mindful, where full attention is given to the ongoing task, results in thoroughness and often quicker task completion. By focusing on the present, we liberate our minds, enabling them to function optimally.

3.2. Key Benefits of a Mindful Approach to Time Management

In the realm of time management, mindfulness paves the way for a gamut of benefits impacting our work, health, and overall life quality.

1. **Improved Focus and Concentration**: With mindfulness, your attention stays locked on the current task, leading to increased productivity.

2. **Reduced Stress**: Mindfulness teaches you to navigate your thoughts rather than being consumed by them. This approach can significantly reduce anxiety related to planning tasks and future time commitments.

3. **Enhanced Decision Making**: Being present enables you to see situations clearly, deciding based on current facts rather than assumptions or past experiences.

4. **Boosted Efficiency**: Mindfulness aids in identifying distractions or time-wasting behaviors, enabling you to utilize your time in a more streamlined and efficient manner.

3.3. Techniques to Cultivate Mindfulness for Time Management

Mindfulness is not innate; it's a skill that gets refined with consistent practice. Here are practical techniques to kick-start your mindfulness journey:

1. **Meditation**: A timeless technique, meditation is renowned for fostering mindfulness. Begin with a few minutes daily, progressively increasing the time spent. This practice helps to center your thoughts and bring conscious awareness to your present.

2. **Awareness Breaks**: Pause during different times of your day, focusing on your sensory experiences. This act could be as simple as savoring your morning coffee or feeling the breeze during a short walk.

3. **Mindful Listening**: Actively listen during conversations. It enhances your engagement levels, strengthens relationships, and allows for more efficient communication.

4. **Single-tasking**: In a world that glorifies multitasking, embrace the simplicity of performing one task at a time. It can significantly improve your productivity and the quality of work.

5. **Keep a Mindfulness Journal**: Dedicate a few minutes at the end of the day to journal about your experiences. It fosters greater self-awareness and aids in identifying patterns that may impact your time management.

3.4. Implementing Mindfulness into Your Time Management Plan

Once mindfulness becomes second nature, integrate it into your time management plan. Start by incorporating it into your scheduling - recognize your most focused hours of the day and assign complex tasks to these periods. Similarly, identify when your energy typically dips and allocate simpler tasks or breaks to these times.

When planning your day, be present and realistic. Overextending leads to stress, while underestimating can breed complacency. Regularly review and reassess your plan, making any necessary adjustments. Remember that flexibility is a pillar of good time management.

While tracking your time, make note of interruptions – an email alert, impromptu meetings, or simply daydreaming. Highlighting these distractions anchors your focus, allowing you to adjust and ensure better time management in the future.

Embracing a mindful approach to time management is an essential first step towards reclaiming command over your life through time. By being present in your decisions and actions, aligning your focus on the task at hand, and successfully separating the past and future from the present, you will find your days becoming progressively more productive, satisfying, and fulfilling. Commence this journey with an open mind, and witness how the simple act of mindfulness can morph ordinary moments into extraordinary achievements.

Chapter 4. Deconstructing Procrastination: The Mindfulness Way

Management sage Peter Drucker once opined, "Time is the scarcest resource, and unless it is managed, nothing else can be managed." For many, the battle against time frequently presents as procrastination, a persistent nemesis sapping productivity and peace. But fear not, with the tools of mindfulness, there exists a pathway to break free from procrastinating chains and reclaim the reins of time.

4.1. Understanding Procrastination

Let's begin with understanding what procrastination is. It's not mere laziness or lack of willpower, as one might think. Procrastination is a complex psychological behavior that arises from the discomfort of starting or completing a task. At its core, procrastination is an emotional management problem where the individual avoids tasks that stir anxiety or discomfort. It's essentially an escape mechanism that temporarily shields us from negative emotions but ultimately backfires, leading to stress, guilt, and loss of productivity.

Research suggests that from a neurological standpoint, procrastination is essentially a tussle between two brain regions - the primitive limbic system, which is impulsive and seeks immediate gratification, and the prefrontal cortex, the 'planner,' which advocates for long-term goals. The limbic system, being evolutionarily older, often proves the more influential of the two.

4.2. Mindfulness: The Procrastination Antidote

Mindfulness, a practice of being consciously aware of the present moment without judgment, carries the potential to disrupt this procrastination cycle. It equips us with the ability to regulate our emotions, thereby reducing the urgency to resort to procrastination.

Tuning into mindfulness allows us to acknowledge the emotions that trigger procrastination without acting upon them. It provides us with a choice, offers a moment of pause to reflect, and make a conscious decision rather than succumbing to impulsivity. With regular practice, mindfulness enhances emotional resilience, helping us to stay focused on the task at hand, free from interference by distracting emotions or thoughts.

4.3. Getting Started with Mindfulness

To leverage mindfulness in combating procrastination, we first need to establish a regular formal mindfulness practice. There are numerous ways to do this, such as mindful breathing, engaging in body scans, or enrolling in mindfulness-based stress reduction (MBSR) programs.

Begin by setting aside at least 10-15 minutes a day to engage in a formal mindfulness practice. Simple exercises like focusing on your breath can be a good start. Gradually, as your mindfulness muscle strengthens, increase your practice duration.

Once you have established a regular formal mindfulness practice, it's time to begin incorporating mindfulness informally into everyday activities.

4.4. Applying Mindfulness to Procrastination: A Step-by-Step Guide

Now that we've laid a solid mindfulness foundation let's dissect how to apply it to curb procrastination. Remember, this isn't a quick fix; but consistent practice can yield transformative results.

1. Identify the task: Start by identifying the task you are procrastinating. Whether it's a looming work assignment, an overdue report, or a long-procrastinated errand, bring it clearly into your mind's focus.

2. Tune into your emotions: Notice the emotions that swell up when you think of this task. Anxiety? Dread? Boredom? Be a neutral observer of the spectrum of your emotions, without judgment.

3. Mindful Breathing: Practice mindful breathing to center yourself in the presence. Remember, the objective here is not to alter your feelings or forcibly relax but simply to notice your natural breath pattern without any judgment.

4. Choose action: Armed with awareness and a refocused mind, consciously choose to act. Take the smallest manageable action towards the task completion.

5. Acknowledge distractions: As you embark on your task, acknowledge that distractions will surface. When they do, simply observe them without judgment and gently bring your focus back to your task.

6. Practice compassion: Mindfulness is about not just awareness but also compassion. So, if you find yourself procrastinating again, don't beat yourself up. Instead, gently guide your focus back to the task, just as you would in a formal mindfulness practice.

7. Celebrate small victories: Every time you overcome a procrastination challenge using mindfulness, celebrate it. This

reinforces the positive behavior, making it more likely that you'll repeat it in the future.

4.5. Embedding Mindfulness in Your Daily Routine

Having an established mindfulness practice and knowing the steps to tackle procrastination is not enough. We must embed mindfulness into our daily habits. To help you achieve this, the below initiatives could be of help.

1. Mindful Mornings: Make mindfulness the first thing in your day. Dedicate 10-15 minutes every morning to a mindfulness exercise.

2. Mindful Breaks: Utilize breaks during your day to engage in short mindfulness practices. Just a few minutes of mindfulness can refresh your mind, improve focus, and keep procrastination at bay.

3. Mindful Transitioning: Use transition periods, such as the time between chores or meetings as opportunities for mindful reflection. This helps in resetting your focus and reduces chances of slipping into procrastination when switching tasks.

4. Mindful Conclusion: End your day with a mindfulness practice. This will help you unwind and prepare your mind for a restful sleep, setting a positive tone for the next day.

In essence, mindfulness can equip us with the tools necessary to tackle procrastination. By being aware of our emotions and triggers, disentangling from them, and choosing our actions consciously, we can reclaim control over our time. As we continually train our minds through mindfulness, we transform procrastination from a daunting obstacle into an opportunity for growth. With time and practice, you will find that mindfulness not only resolves procrastination but also instills a deeper sense of peace and satisfaction within your daily life. Remember, the journey of mastering time is also the path towards mastering your life.

Chapter 5. Essential Time Management Techniques: Tools of Empowerment

Time is an unchanging constant that moves regardless of our actions. By effectively implementing time management techniques, we can become masters of our own time, increasing productivity and overall life satisfaction. These empowering tools are the foundation towards a future where time is an ally, not a foe.

5.1. The Power of Prioritization

The first technique to reclaim your time is understanding and implementing the power of prioritization. This tool is valuable as it helps steer your focus towards tasks that are vital and yield high results.

Quadrant of Prioritization: Old but gold, this tool was introduced by Stephen Covey in his book 'The 7 Habits of Highly Effective People'. He champions the idea that tasks can be divided into four quadrants based on their urgency and importance: 1. Urgent and Important 2. Not Urgent but Important 3. Urgent but Not Important 4. Not Urgent and Not Important

After organizing your tasks into these categories, focus primarily on those in the 'Not Urgent but Important' category, as these contribute most significantly towards your long-term goals.

5.2. The Eisenhower Matrix

Akin to Covey's Quadrants, the Eisenhower Matrix stems from a quote by former US President Dwight D. Eisenhower: "What is important is seldom urgent and what is urgent is seldom important." The matrix categorizes tasks into: 1. Urgent and Important (Do it now) 2. Important but Not Urgent (Schedule it) 3. Urgent but Not Important (Delegate it) 4. Neither Urgent nor Important (Delete it)

The primary differential between the two models is that Eisenhower's Matrix recommends actions for each category, promoting proactive time management.

5.3. Time Blocking

Time blocking is the practice of setting a specific time frame for a particular task or set of tasks. It creates structure, channels focus, and reduces the threat of multitasking – a common efficiency killer.

Steps to Effective Time Blocking: - Identify your top priorities. - Consider your high-energy periods during the day. - Block out time on your calendar for executing these tasks. - Defend your blocks and prevent external factors from invading them.

5.4. The Pomodoro Technique

The Pomodoro Technique involves breaking your work sessions into manageable 25-minute chunks - called 'Pomodoros,' followed by 5-minute breaks. After every fourth Pomodoro, take a longer break of 15-20 minutes. Francesco Cirillo, the inventor of this technique, advocates for its assistance in combating burnout and promoting sustained concentration.

5.5. The 80/20 Rule or Pareto Principle

Economist Vilfredo Pareto determined that roughly 80% of the results come from 20% of the efforts. Implementing this principle into your time management pushes you to identify that crucial 20% that stimulates the maximum productivity. Prioritize these tasks to drive effective outcomes.

5.6. Goal Setting: SMART Goals

In time management, goal setting is paramount. SMART Goals, an acronym for Specific, Measurable, Attainable, Relevant, and Time-bound, give a clear direction as they are well-defined and time-oriented. They redirect focus and enable a streamlined approach towards productivity.

5.7. The Power of Delegation

Delegation is a potent time management tool that empowers you to share tasks, providing more time to focus on high-priority actions. The key to effective delegation iÅs trust and clear communication. It's not just about transferring tasks, but more about team participation and skill development.

5.8. The Art of Saying No

Learning to refuse added responsibilities or unnecessary tasks saves significant time. It reaffirms the value of your time and keeps you from getting overwhelmed. Being assertive without sounding arrogant is an art that is essential to master.

These various strategies offer a comprehensive arsenal of time management tools to employ. Each is powerful and beneficial in its way, yet finding which one or combination works best for you involves trial and error. Remember, the goal is not to create a regimented, minute-by-minute schedule, but to construct an empowering, flexible routine that enhances productivity and introduces tranquility into your daily life. The key to successful time management isn't about chasing seconds, but about controlling your actions, thereby becoming the master of your time.

Chapter 6. Shifting Gears: Transitioning to a Mindful Schedule

The act of shifting gears signifies embracing change. Just as a car smoothly switches gears to adapt to the road's circumstances, we too must learn to transition our schedules, integrating mindfulness for a richer, fuller life. Mastering such a transition involves understanding mindfulness, analyzing your existing routine, and discovering effective strategies to incorporate these concepts into your schedule.

6.1. Understanding Mindfulness

Mindfulness may have its roots in Buddhist meditation, but its application extends to secular practices today. At its core, mindfulness is the practice of living in the present moment, consciously and fully aware of your emotions, thoughts and actions without criticism or judgment. It encourages one to acknowledge and accept feelings, enhancing one's relationship with oneself and the surrounding world through an attitude of openness and curiosity.

Modern science attests to mindfulness's impact on various aspects of life. From boosting mental health, enhancing cognitive abilities, to increasing overall contentment, mindfulness can transform your perception towards life. It fosters resilience, enabling you to navigate life's ups and downs with grace, and patience. However, integrating mindfulness into your routine requires careful planning and dedication.

6.2. Evaluating Your Current Routine

The first step towards transitioning to a mindful schedule is understanding your present routine. It's like laying the land bare before planting a new crop. Take a few days to journal every activity you undertake from the minute you wake up to when you retire for the night. Track the time you spend on each task, the breaks you take, the distractions you succumb to, and how you feel throughout the day.

Understanding your patterns, the highs and lows of your energy, moods, and productivity levels can reveal insights into how best to structure your day. Look for patterns and gaps where mindfulness activities can be integrated to enhance not just productivity but also overall well-being.

6.3. Mindfulness Activities and Their Integration

Table 1. Mindful Activities and Related Time Slots

Mindful Activities	Best Time Slots
Meditation	Early morning or before bedtime
Mindful Eating	During meals
Single-tasking	Throughout the day
Daily Reflection	End of the day

Mindfulness activities range from meditation, mindful eating, single-tasking to daily reflection, and more. Each has unique benefits that can enrich your life. Scheduling these activities into appropriate time slots can ensure successful integration.

Meditation, for instance, is a practice that quietens the mind, curbs overwhelm, and nurtures focus and clarity. It's best performed in the early morning or before bedtime when distractions are minimal. Even just ten minutes of daily meditation can be transformative. Various guided meditation apps and programs can aid you in this journey.

Mindful eating, on the other hand, is the practice of eating with attention and without distractions. It promotes healthier eating habits, enhances enjoyment of food, and fosters a better relationship with food. Make it a point to allocate distraction-free time for your meals.

Single-tasking is a cornerstone of mindfulness. Despite the glorification of multitasking, focusing on one task at a time boosts productivity and reduces stress. It ensures you give your full attention to the task, increasing its quality, and the satisfaction derived from it.

Lastly, *daily reflection* is a powerful tool that strengthens self-awareness. It involves reviewing your day, acknowledging your accomplishments and emotions, and noting points of improvement. Best practised at the end of the day, it becomes a conduit for self-improvement and growth.

6.4. Creating a Mindful Schedule

Once you understand your existing routine and the mindfulness activities you'd like to incorporate, it's time to merge the two. Start small with a few minutes of mindfulness practice per day, gradually increasing as time proceeds.

Maintain flexibility in your routine, allowing the schedule to adapt along with lifestyle changes, but ensure the system's integrity remains. A highly rigid plan might not give the desired results and may even elevate stress levels instead of alleviating them.

In a digitally dominated world, numerous apps can help you in your journey towards developing a mindful schedule. They offer tools to track time, set reminders for mindful activities, and even provide guided programs for practices such as meditation.

It's equally important to remember that while a mindful schedule aims to enhance productivity, its core purpose is to nurture peace of mind. So if a specific strategy feels overwhelming, reassess and revise. After all, the aim is not to become slaves to a routine but masters of our life and time.

6.5. Nurturing a Mindful Lifestyle

A mindful schedule is not a destination but a journey towards a more fulfilling life. It is a process of continuous improvement and self-exploration. As you navigate through this path, you'll discover unique wisdom about yourself, your preferences, and the kind of life that brings you joy.

Remember, the essence of mindfulness lies in understanding, acceptance, and love for oneself and life on a profound level. By aligning your schedule with mindfulness practices, you are setting the stage for greater peace, fulfillment, and a life that resonates with the rhythm of your true self. It's about making friends with time and learning to dance to its beat.

By diligently applying these strategies, your relationship with time will shift. While time remains constant and unchanging, your perception of it transforms. It becomes a friend and ally, a canvas upon which you paint your lifetime masterpiece. The magic unveiled through this transition is your key to unlocking a life of enhanced productivity balanced with serene mindfulness.

Chapter 7. Productivity and Peace: Balancing Act of Time Management

Time management and productivity are two peaks on the same mountain. The path intertwining both presents a most engaging challenge. The marriage of productivity and peace of mind through efficient time management dispels the myth that 'busy' equates to productive. Embark on a journey, blending sheer productivity with inner tranquility.

7.1. The Paradox: Busy vs. Productive

Busyness is often mistaken for productivity, yet both are as different as rushing water and still lake. Being 'busy' doesn't necessarily translate to being fruitful. Many times, we involve ourselves in low-impact tasks, contributing minimally towards our goals, while overlooking significant tasks that can bring substantial progress.

To unlock the true power of productivity, you must approach it with a peace of mind. It's not about how full your schedule is, but more about how fruitful your efforts are. Therefore, identifying high-impact tasks and focusing on those tasks within a defined time frame can help ensure meaningful productivity.

7.2. Productivity Quadrant: Identifying High Impact Tasks

Consider this while identifying high-impact tasks: There are essentially four categories every task falls into.

1. Urgent and Essential

2. Important but Not Urgent

3. Urgent but Not Important

4. Neither Urgent nor Important

The secret of high productivity lies in the ability to distinguish between 'Important' tasks and 'Urgent' tasks. Urgent tasks demand immediate attention, while important tasks contribute to your long-term mission, values, and goals. Evaluate and identify tasks essential for your productivity and invest quality time in accomplishing them.

7.3. Time Blocking: Structuring Productivity

Time blocking, a simple yet highly productive time management technique, lets you assign specific time slots for different tasks throughout your day. It creates a visual representation of your time, enabling more effective planning.

1. Identify your high-impact tasks, ruthlessly prioritize, and estimate the time each task will require.

2. Break your tasks into manageable parts; this keeps your schedule flexible and adaptable.

3. Assign each task to a specific time block. Focus solely on the task within that time, free from interruptions.

4. Keep track of your time blocks. Learn, refine, and adjust your schedule based on your productivity levels.

7.4. The Art of Mindful Productivity

Mindfulness plays a pivotal role in bolstering productivity. By focusing on the present, it reduces anxiety, stress, and the feeling of being overwhelmed. Moreover, it proves invaluable in fostering a sense of inner peace and calm that enhances productivity.

Practicing mindfulness while executing tasks can significantly increase your efficiency. Engage wholly in the task, notice every detail without any rush, and appreciate your progress. Immutable focus fosters clearer thinking, and thoughts are steps on the path to productivity and peace.

7.5. Combining Peace and Productivity

Once you grasp the concepts of productive time management and mindful execution, the next step is to merge these aspects harmoniously. The convergence of mindfulness and productivity triggers a magical alignment leading to substantial progress.

- Start your day by setting intentions. Map out your tasks and plan your day. But, also, take a moment to meditate and create a calm mental space.

- During the day, tune into your tasks fully. Appreciate your efforts, irrespective of the result.

- Take short mindfulness breaks. This offers a chance to relax, rejuvenate, and reframe your mind.

- Evaluate your day's work in the light of mindfulness. Evoke a sense of gratitude for what you achieved and acceptance for what you could not.

7.6. The Promise of Inner Peace and Productivity

Life is a dance of balance. A regular and systematic fine-tuning of mindful productivity can manifest into sustainable peace and soaring productivity levels over time. As you move forward in your journey, remember that the ultimate goal is not to be incessantly productive but to enjoy productivity meshed with peace.

Mastering the art of mindful productivity and efficient time management is akin to taming a wild river into a placid lake. The potential of time no longer remains constrained like the raging river but becomes a generous friend like the calm lake, brimming with possibilities. A world where productivity is not a tormenting necessity but a tranquil journey filled with mindful moments - that's the world you step into as you embrace this balancing act of time management.

Through trials, triumphs, recalibrations, and revelations, the balance between productivity and peace becomes achievable. It's an arduous journey, no doubt, but one that aligns your time and energy with the rhythm of peace and productiveness. This way, time management does not remain a mere organizational tool. Instead, it transforms into a life strategy, a constant companion in your quest for fruitful productivity and tranquil peace.

In the grand scheme of existence, time is neutral, its power determined by how it is wielded. The apt blend of productive time management and mindful presence has potential not merely to enhance your relationship with time but to redefine it - from an enemy to an ally, from constraint to possibility.

Chapter 8. Saying No Graciously: The Art of Mindful Delegation

Mastering the art of mindful delegation begins with a simple, but often overlooked, element of communication—saying "No" graciously. This powerful two-letter word has the capacity to recalibrate time, resources, and attention, allowing us to focus on the most critical tasks. However, saying "No" is just one part of the equation. Delegating tasks effectively is equally important to take full advantage of the value of your time.

8.1. Acknowledging the Power of 'No'

The idea of saying 'No' often connotes negation and rejection, but in reality, it's more about boundary-setting and self-respect. Whether you're a manager juggling numerous responsibilities or an individual snowed under a mountain of tasks, saying 'No' is a tool to sift through the noise and prioritize what genuinely matters.

Many find refusal difficult because they fear it will signal incompetence, uncooperativeness, or selfishness. However, saying 'No' is not an act of rejection, but one of selection. It's distinguishing between the critical few and trivial many, thus helping you focus on tasks that yield the most significant benefits and align with personal or organization's goals.

Importantly, how you communicate the 'No' is crucial. It should be polite and respectful, acknowledging the requester's needs but also the constraints on your time and attention.

"When approached with a task, instead of an immediate 'Yes' or 'No', strive for an informed decision, considering your current priorities, resource capacity, and the task's alignment with your goals."

8.2. The Role of Mindful Delegation

Delegation is the art of entrusting tasks to others not just for the sake of offloading work, but for efficiency and productivity. It's a strategy to ensure the most capable hands take on the right tasks. Mindful delegation, then, involves careful thought and consideration, assigning duties based on individual capabilities, potential for growth, and the overall team balance.

"Mindful delegation can be compared to solving a puzzle; the objective is not to simply fit the pieces together, but to do so in a way that creates a coherent and harmonious picture."

Not every task can be delegated, but once you've filtered through your tasks and identified what can be reallocated, it's crucial to delegate in a way that empowers your team and contributes to their professional development.

8.3. Constructive Refusal and Empowering Delegation: The Balance

Every 'No' should be followed by a proactive redirection of the task to someone else. This process is a blend of mindful refusal and delegation. Consider the following steps:

1. Evaluate the request: Is it urgent? Who is the best fit to perform this job?

2. Assess capacity: Do you or the person you're considering for

delegation have the bandwidth to take on this task?

3. Communicate: Express your inability with respect, and if you're delegating the task, let the person know why you've chosen them, giving context about the task and its importance.

4. Support: Ensure the person you're delegating to has the necessary resources and your support to complete the task.

8.4. Delegation Done Right: Tips for Success

Proper delegation is about creating a win-win situation. Here are some tips to do it right:

- Explicitly define responsibilities: Clearly articulate the expected results, providing all the necessary information.

- Match tasks with skills: Assign tasks based on each member's strengths and potential for growth.

- Encourage and accept feedback: Open lines of communication, welcoming suggestions and criticism.

- Foster a supportive environment: Display trust in your team's abilities and provide assistance when needed.

- Review progress: Regularly monitor and review task progress, offering constructive feedback and assistance.

By learning to say 'No' graciously and delegate tasks mindfully, not only can you manage your time effectively, but also foster a more productive and harmonious working environment. This area of skill truly is a vocational virtue, blending efficiency, respect, growth, and team harmony, offering an innovative answer to the timeless challenge of time management. It's in this intricate dance of refusal and delegation where your ally, Time, truly shines. Match the rhythm, and enjoy the dance!

Chapter 9. Life beyond To-Do Lists: Mindfulness in Daily Chores

The constant glare of staggering to-do lists can seem overwhelming at times. When these lists expand and conquer your day, time becomes a prisoner of chores. However, there's a path less traveled — a journey of mindfulness imbued within the mundane. This transformative approach is about blending, not battling. It converges seemingly disparate elements: the frantic pace of activities on one hand and tranquil mindfulness on the other.

9.1. The Power of Mindful Doing

Let's commence from understanding the 'how' before we move on to the 'why'. Mindful doing is more than just an act; it's an experience — a shift from unconscious autopiloting to conscious awareness. Imagine doing dishes; instead of rushing through the task while mentally preparing for the next one, you immerse yourself in the experience — the feel of the sponge, the sound of running water, the sight of bubbles clinging onto the plate. Your mind is present, focused, and free from the buzzing anxiety of what's to come.

Being fully present in mundane tasks fosters a sense of peace, gratitude, and calmness that transcends the ordinary and imparts a quality of meditation to the work. When dissected, the phrase "mindful doing" reveals its core essence — to perform each task with complete mindfulness or "full-mindedness", a state where all your attention is encapsulated within the task, freeing you from the cobwebs of past regrets or future worries.

9.2. Mindfulness Over Multitasking

Multitasking has been heavily lauded in our fast-paced society. It's seen as a virtue of efficiency, a mark of productivity. However, scientific findings reveal an entirely different narrative. Multitasking, in fact, diminishes productivity by up to 40%, impedes cognitive function and drains mental energy. On the contrary, practicing mindfulness enhances concentration, retention, and job satisfaction while reducing stress levels.

Strive to embrace single-tasking with complete focus and attention. Letter by letter, word by word, task by task - the beauty lies in the deep and undivided attention that you offer to every mundane act. This is mindfulness in action, your stepping stone to an enriching life beyond to-do lists.

9.3. The Science Backs the Benefits

Mindfulness is not a metaphysical practice unrooted from reality; it is firmly anchored in science. Neuroscientific research has shown that regular mindfulness exercises lead to an increase in grey matter in the prefrontal cortex, an area responsible for executive function like decision making and self-regulation.

On the physiological front, mindfulness exercises reduce stress hormone cortisol levels, improve the quality of sleep, lower blood pressure, and boost the immune system. From a psychological lens, it enhances emotional well-being, lowers symptoms of depression and anxiety, and increases overall life satisfaction. Introducing mindfulness in daily chores is not a luxury; it's an essential ingredient for a wholesome life.

9.4. Anchoring Mindfulness in Daily Chores

Starting from the very first act of your day — waking up — make a conscious effort to be present. Feel the softness of your bed, listen to the chirping of birds, sense the warmth of the morning sun on your skin. When brushing your teeth, instead of navigating through your day in your head, focus on the strokes, the taste of the toothpaste, the rhythm of the act.

Inculcate this practice into each task, no matter how mundane — be it drinking your coffee, making breakfast, or taking a shower. Cultivate an appreciation for these small acts of living. This exercise effectively bottles down to shifting from "doing mode" to "being mode." Here, you're not aiming for efficiency or speed, but ingraining a sense of deep connectedness and tranquility in everyday life.

9.5. From Theory to Reality

Implementing mindfulness may seem challenging initially. With racing thoughts constantly intruding, maintaining focus could be laborious. However, like any other skill, it requires practice. Guided mindfulness practices and apps can offer a good start.

Start with brief pockets of mindfulness, and gradually extend them. Perfection is not the goal; persistent effort is. If your mind wanders, judgements may cloud over, triggering feelings of failure. Remember, these are mere hiccups, not halt signs; gently bring your focus back over and over again.

9.6. Life's Hidden Meditation

Viewing chores as meditative practices can profoundly alter our relationship with them. Sometimes, life's simplest tasks can be venues for the most profound experiences. They can be gateways to stillness, a respite from the chaos, and an opportunity to build a loving relationship with the present moment.

Make every small task a mini-meditation - your chance to bask in the 'nowness' of life. Witness the transformation as your daily chores, once seen as time-stealing burdens, metamorphose into pulsating moments of life that you look forward to each day.

In the end, mindfulness in daily chores is a beautiful journey from stress to serenity, from 'doing' to 'being', and from time as a foe to time as a friend. It provides a palette to paint ordinary tasks with extraordinary hues of joy, tranquility, and poise. Through the integration of mindfulness in daily chores, life ceases to be a series of tasks to be accomplished, and instead, becomes a journey to be thoroughly cherished.

Chapter 10. Time Mindfulness in Digital Age: Managing Screen Time

In the era of technological innovation, our reliance on digital devices has drastically increased. From smartphones to smart homes, digital screens dictate our daily routines, habits, and productivity, often blurring the lines between work and relaxation periods. Managing screen time becomes a crucial aspect of creating a balanced, healthy, and mindful lifestyle. The following sections detail hands-on strategies for effective screen time management combined with mindfulness in the digital age.

10.1. The Screen Time Conundrum

Screens permeate every facet of our life – work, leisure, communication, navigation, information – to mention a few. While they undoubtedly enhance productivity and offer a world of knowledge at our fingertips, they also cast a shadow of excessive usage, compromised health, and strained relationships. It is not uncommon for individuals, after a long day swiping through emails, messages, or scrolling social media, to feel drained, anxious, and unproductive.

The Pew Research Center states that about 28% of Americans report going online "almost constantly," with 45% doing so multiple times a day. Physiological issues like eye strain, insomnia, and obesity aside, uncontrolled screen time can lead to psychological problems such as addiction, depression, and anxiety.

Therefore, the challenge is to use technology to our advantage rather than falling prey to its detrimental facets. Shift the narrative from being controlled by screens to controlling them, and from mindless consumption to mindful interaction.

10.2. Unveiling the Mindful Approach to Screen Time

Mindfulness, the practice of paying attention purposefully in the present moment and non-judgmentally, is a powerful tool to wield in managing screen time. It steers us from being lost in the digital world to being conscious of our engagement with it.

A mindful approach to screen time isn't about drastic measures like digital detoxes or tech-free days alone. It revolves around being aware and deliberative with digital interactions – noticing when, how, and why we reach for gadgets, being present during screen time, and consciously deciding when to switch off. It transforms screen time from a mindless habit to an intentional act.

10.3. Practical Strategies for Mindful Screen Time

1. Awareness: The first step towards change is always awareness. Monitor your current screen time using inbuilt settings on most devices, or download apps aimed at tracking digital usage. You might be startled to find the extent of your unconscious screen engagement.

2. Set Clear Boundaries: Schedule specific 'technology-free' times or 'mindful tech' times throughout the day. This could be during meals, before bedtime, or the first hour after waking. Reclaim these moments for personal mental space, physical activity or connection with others.

3. Single-Tasking: Our brains are not wired to multitask effectively. Combat digital distractions by practicing single-tasking. Dedicate specific slots for checking emails, social media, or other digital

tasks. During these slots, just do one task at a time, doing it completely and mindfully.

4. Conscious Connection: Before engaging with a digital device, pause and ask yourself – "Why am I reaching for this?", "What am I intending to do?", and "How long do I want to spend?" This creates a mindful space between impulse and action.

5. Digital Environment Design: Creating a supportive digital environment can significantly reduce mindless scrolling and time wasted on unproductive apps. You can rearrange apps on your devices, unsubscribing from unnecessary notifications or decluttering your digital workspace.

10.4. Supercharging Productivity with Mindful Screen Time

Mindful screen time can supercharge productivity by eliminating unnecessary digital distractions, fostering focus, and enhancing digital efficacy. It encourages discernment between the essential and nonessential screen interactions, allowing more time for high-impact activities. It also prevents technology burnout, maintaining our energy levels and enhancing overall digital satisfaction.

Indeed, the digital age presents a challenge that our ancestors did not contend with. However, equipping ourselves with mindfulness can make us the masters of our digital domains, influencing screen time to enhance our lives and not diminish them. Mindful navigation of the digital universe lets us harvest the benefits of technology, tethered to our well-being and personal and professional growth.

Remember, it is not the technology but how we use it that dictates our experience. So, let's redefine our relationship with screen time, swapping mindless consumption for mindful interaction, and transforming screen time from a daunting conceptual figure to an amicable ally in our digital age journey. Let's unlock the magic of time mindfulness and reclaim our lives!

Chapter 11. Recap and Moving Ahead: Cultivating a Mindful Time Management Habit

The journey you've embarked upon in the preceding pages is one of significance, rife with revelations and understandings about the intricate amalgamation of time management and mindfulness. As you revisit the concepts learned, strategies adopted, and habits fostered, you'll begin to see an evolving pattern in your life. One of enhanced productivity, calmer responses to challenging situations, and, most importantly, improved self-awareness.

11.1. Taking Stock of The Learned Concepts

v Unveiling the Mask of Time: This adventure began with demystifying time. Time isn't merely linear or cyclical but a blend of both, with profound psychological implications. Your investigation into the influence of clock-time (Chronos) and significant or experiential time (Kairos) painted a complex picture of how you interface with time.

v Mindfulness Decoder: Diving into the essence of mindfulness, you uncovered its phenomenal capabilities. Not just a transient fad, mindfulness is an ancient practice swelling with benefits.

v The Unseen Link: You participated in the unveiling of a hidden connection–between time management and mindfulness. You discovered how this potent blend paves the way for a life centered on productivity, peace, and purpose.

11.2. Adopted Strategies: A Recap

Throughout this journey, several strategies have been introduced. Each tailored to craft a healthier mindset towards time.

v Adopting Time Blocking: By segmenting your day into manageable blocks dedicated to specific tasks, you conquer the tyranny of an uncontrolled time.

v Creating Time: By identifying time vampires like excessive screen-time, you unlocked opportunities to recoup several hours each week.

v Taking Mindful Pauses: Regular time-outs for mindful breathing exercises or meditation sessions fueled a decrease in pressure, facilitating a more attention-focused processing of time.

v Mindful Planning: By embracing a thoughtful approach to planning, where intention drove your actions, you soared above the chaotic waves of haste and haste-driven mistakes.

v Environmental Shifts: Simplifying your space, decluttering, and creating an environment conducive to focus and productivity nudged you to maximise your time.

11.3. Cultivating Mindful Habits

As you process the comprehensive strategy ensemble, it's crucial to understand that invariably, it's consistent practice that brings transformation. Seldom does change occur overnight.

By cultivating these mindful habits, the delicate balance of time management and mindfulness can be achieved and maintained:

1. Love your Calendar: Updating, and regularly referring to, your calendar is an essential ingredient for effective time management.

2. Mindful Rising: Start your day with intentionality. A morning routine, infused with mindfulness, paves the way for the remainder of the day.

3. Pause and Breathe: Remember to take periodic breaks. Use them as moments for mindfulness, grounding yourself in the present.

4. Gratitude and Reflection: End your day by acknowledging your achievements, however big or small. A sense of gratitude fosters contentment.

5. Regular Detox: Designate a day for digital detox. Time away from digital devices promotes a more conscious interaction with time.

11.4. Transformation Takes Time

The ethos of this transformation revolves around the word "time" itself. Understanding that every change takes time will help you stay patient and persistent. Harness the newfound knowledge, experiment with different strategies, and give yourself ample room to evolve. The fulfilling journey of blending mindfulness and time management requires time. It doesn't demand perfect execution–only your persistence, patience, and mindfulness.

Remember to celebrate your progress, no matter how insignificant the steps might seem. After all, a journey of a thousand miles begins with a single step, and each mindful step you take is a step towards a more aware, productive, and fulfilling life.